NEWPORT BUS

SIMON INGHAM

AMBERLEY

First published 2026

Amberley Publishing
The Hill, Stroud
Gloucestershire, GL5 4EP

www.amberley-books.com

Copyright © Simon Ingham, 2026

The right of Simon Ingham to be identified as the Author of this work has been asserted in accordance with the Copyrights, Designs and Patents Act 1988.

ISBN 978 1 3981 0928 5 (print)
ISBN 978 1 3981 0929 2 (ebook)

British Library Cataloguing in Publication Data.
A catalogue record for this book is available from the British Library.

Typesetting by SJmagic DESIGN SERVICES, India.
Printed in the UK.

Appointed GPSR EU Representative: Easy Access System Europe Oü, 16879218
Address: Mustamäe tee 50, 10621, Tallinn, Estonia
Contact Details: gpsr.requests@easproject.com, +358 40 500 3575

Contents

Foreword

As Managing Director of Newport Transport, it is my pleasure to be writing this foreword.

It is a proud moment in the company's history; we are approaching 125 years since Newport Corporation took over the town's horse-drawn bus service and established a municipal bus operation. The company has seen some significant changes since then in terms of geographical area covered, technology, staff and vehicles. One thing remains unchanged, however: our dedication to delivering a quality, affordable and reliable service to our customers and communities.

Our local bus network now operates in ten local authority areas, stretching across Cardiff, Hereford, the Forest of Dean and Bristol, as well as providing a comprehensive network in our home city. We have a strong private-hire business under the brand Newport Coach and a successful partnership with FlixBus.

Our vehicles have long been known to be green in colour, but our fleet has grown to become one of the cleanest, greenest, environmentally friendly fleets in the UK with the introduction of Yutong electric vehicles.

We have various celebrations planned for our 125th anniversary in 2026 and I hope that you can join us to mark our milestone in some way. I'm forever grateful for the support and commitment from our staff, past and present, for their contributions in making Newport Transport what it is today. Thank you to the people of Newport for your continued support and to Simon for his hard work and enthusiasm in creating this book.

Morgan Stevens, Newport Transport MD

Introduction

The release of this publication in 2026 is significant as this year marks the 125th anniversary of Newport Corporation, the forerunner to Newport Transport and Newport Bus, taking over responsibility of the town's public transport system. The transfer happened at midnight on Saturday 30 July 1901. 2026 also marks 102 years since the first motor bus service commenced in Newport. This was between Clarence Place (Rodney Road) and Gibbs Road (Christchurch), launching on 7 April 1924 with a 20-minute frequency. It was also 100 years ago, around 1926, that pneumatic tyres replaced solid tyres on buses, a progressive step in the history of public transport that should also be noted, if not celebrated.

All pictures used in this publication have been taken by myself, Simon Ingham, in the years leading up to 2026 as a milestone year for Newport Transport. The pictures appear in fleet number and date order, with a selection of the coach fleet, demonstrators and preserved vehicles as well as bus interiors, station and depot shots at the back of the book. Combined, they give a flavour of the changing scene of Newport Bus up to and including the introduction of zero-tailpipe-emission electric vehicles. At the beginning of 2026, there were fifty-nine examples in the bus fleet (eleven Yutong E9Ls, eighteen Yutong E10s, twenty-eight Yutong E12s and two Yutong U11DDs), with a further six in the coach fleet in the form of Yutong TCe12s. Diesel single-deck vehicles include one active Scania OmniCity, three Mercedes-Benz Sprinter EVM Citylines, five ADL Enviro200s and six ADL Enviro200 MMCs. Diesel double-deck vehicles include one active Dennis Trident East Lancs Myllennium Lolyne, four Dennis Trident Plaxton Presidents, six ADL Enviro400 MMCs, seven ADL Enviro400s and eleven Dennis Trident Alexander ALX400s. The active coach fleet consists of one AOS Grand Touro C35F, one Yutong TC9, one Volvo Plaxton Elite, one DAF Van Hool, three Scania Irizars, five Volvo Plaxton Panthers, five Mercedes-Benz Tourismos, eight Volvo 9700s and eight Yutong GT12s. There are further minibuses in the fleet and multiple preserved ex-Newport vehicles exist, some of which are in the care of Newport Bus and reside at the Corporation Road Depot.

The livery of Newport Bus has long been associated with the colour green. The shade of green used from 1937 to 1998 has often been referred to as 'leaf green'. A darker green was introduced in 1998 when the first low-floor buses were brought in. In 2009, a livery variation was introduced when the ex-Lothian Volvo Olympians arrived. This livery morphed into another variation in 2010 for the single-deck fleet with a large 'N' logo applied to the rear of vehicles and headlight surrounds finished with lime green paintwork. In 2012, the dark green was replaced by a lighter shade. The double-deckers had adopted their own livery that differed from the single-deckers. In 2017, the livery adopted was all-over green, like that worn by the X30-branded Scania OmniCitys new in 2011. The electrics of 2020 and beyond arrived in a lighter 'Yutong' shade of green. This allows for quick differentiation between diesel and zero-tailpipe-emission vehicles.

For an in-depth look at the history and fleet of the company, Andrew Wiltshire's *Newport's Municipal Buses* (2021) is a great source, as well as older publications such as D. B. Thomas and E. A. Thomas's 1982 release *Trams and Buses of Newport 1845 to 1981*, E. A. Thomas's

Newport Transport – 80 Years of Service (1981) and the *Newport Transport Centenary* booklet from 2001. Bustimes.org, Bus Lists on the Web and Chris Meaker's web summary of the fleet have been invaluable in the collation of information included within on the more contemporary Newport Bus business. Extended thanks must go to Alex Clarke and the Management Team at Newport Transport for access to information and records, as well as their stamp of approval for this book's publication during such a significant year for the company.

Taken on 2 September 2003, aged twelve. I was about to board Leyland Atlantean ATK 154W for an open-top bus ride around my home city. Little did I know that some twenty-three years later I'd be the author of a book about Newport Bus.

Newport Bus

Scania OmniCity YN57 FZT (1) is captured resting in the Newport Bus Depot on 8 April 2021. It would later become a driver trainer, wearing a yellow base livery. This was one of twelve new in 2007, three with 07-plates and nine with 57-plates.

Scania OmniCity YN57 FZU (2) turning into Newport Bus Station on a foggy day in December 2010 after completing an X30 service from the Welsh capital. Seen in the background is the newly built University of South Wales Riverside Campus.

A June 2010 shot of Scania OmniCity YN57 FZV (3) in the traditional green and cream livery. The Newport City Footbridge is visible behind, which links the east bank of the river in the vicinity of Rodney Parade stadium to University Plaza on the west bank. Its structure has symbolic links to the site's earlier use as a trading wharf.

On 16 July 2022, YN57 FZV (3) is captured exiting the bus station on the 15, Bettws Circular. It is wearing the all-over black and amber colours of Newport County, one of three vehicles to wear such livery, though not simultaneously, the others being Alexander Dennis Enviro200 YX11 AHV (306) and Wright Meridian CN60 FBO (101).

YN57 FZY (6) is seen in Cwmbran Bus Station about to depart back to Newport. It passes Stagecoach South Wales Alexander ALX200 Dennis Dart SLF R451 FVX (34051), which was new to East London in May 1998 as SLD51.

Scania Wright Access Floline S110 TDW (10) is seen preparing to work service 1A to Rogerstone in August 2012. Prior to withdrawal, it operated in plain white livery with Newport Bus fleet names. None of the batch survived to make it into later Newport Bus liveries.

S112 TDW (12) is seen passing Newport's *Steel Wave*, nearly completing the morning run of service 18. Daffodils are seen in bloom, which is apt as the date is 2 March 2013.

S114 TDW (14) is captured on 22 June 2010 in the more traditional livery having worked the 26C service.

A May 2012 shot of S117 TDW (17) about to turn to face the opposite direction and layover at Newport Bus Station, similar to Scania OmniCity YN07 VCO (51) behind, having worked the 30 service from Cardiff.

S118 TDW (18) is working the 18 service from Malpas, captured in High Street on 10 December 2011. Numerically, this was the last of nine new to Newport in September 1998, numbered 11 to 18 inclusively.

Y32 GBO (32) was one of six Y-registered Alexander ALX200-bodied Dennis Dart SLFs delivered new to Newport Bus in May 2001. The others were Y131 GBO (31), Y133 GBO (33), Y134 GBO (34), Y84 GBO (84) and Y185 GBO (85); the other five in the fleet were W-registered examples. Y32 GBO (32) is seen on the Town Circular service 4 on 6 April 2013 being followed to the bus station by Scania OmniCity YN53 GGX (59).

Numerically the first in the back of six Dennis Tridents new to Newport with ALX400 bodywork (numbered 35–40 inclusive), V35HTG (35) received an all-over festive wrap in 2011 wishing Newport Bus customers a Merry Christmas and Happy New Year. It is seen in Newport Bus Station on 17 December of that year. Logos from supporting sponsors include CBS Outdoor, Parkeon, Freshwater, Pennine Signs, Alexander Dennis and Scania.

V36 HTG (36) seen in the more traditional green and cream livery in Newport Bus Station on 23 April 2011. Earlier in its life it wore two-tone red and blue advertising livery for Acorn Recruitment.

An October 2013 shot of Dennis Trident with Alexander ALX400 bodywork V37 HTG (37) negotiating the winding entrance to Newport Bus Station as a result of works associated with the building of the new Friars Walk complex. It is seen having finished a run on service 16 in between a winter shower.

V39 HTG (39) leaves Newport Bus Station on a service 17 to Malpas on 25 October 2013. Like others in this batch, when new it wore a large vinyl of the *Steel Wave* applied to the side with the large 'Newport Transport' fleet name between the saloons. This vehicle was created in model form by Create Master Northcord as their UKBUS1011.

Last in the batch numerically with fleet number 40, V140 HTG, a Dennis Trident with Alexander ALX400 bodywork, is seen exiting the Market Square Bus Station in October 2015 on service 42 to Spytty Park. It passes resting Dennis Trident with Plaxton President bodywork LN51 KXV (422). The latter came to Newport second-hand, being new to Metroline as their TPL242 in February 2002.

Scania OmniCity YN54 AOA (41) carrying an all-over advertisement for bmibaby.com is captured entering Newport Bus Station having worked service 8 on 29 December 2010. It is numerically the first of six 54-plate examples delivered to Newport, numbered 41–46 inclusively.

YN54 AOB (42) is seen in July 2013 with its blind set for service 18 to Malpas. The road system along the A4042 was altered, allowing buses to make this right-hand turn from the bus station as opposed to using the Old Green Roundabout. Construction is underway for the Market Square Bus Station to the rear right of the bus. Creative Master Northcord produced a model of this bus in its traditional green and cream livery as UK7001.

YN54 AOC (43) is seen leaving Cwmbran Bus Station onto Glyndwr Road as it begins its journey on service 29B back to Newport in October 2015. It wears an offside advertisement for changes to Welsh Organ Donation later in that year. Behind, the Leisure Cwmbran complex holds the Vue cinema, Frankie & Benny's and Lamare Lebanese Grill among others.

YN54 AOD (44) enters Newport Bus Station in April 2018 after finishing a run back from Cardiff on the 30 service on 28 April 2018. New Adventure Travel's MAN EcoCity OV63 XDD would serve the Market Square Bus Station before continuing on to Ringland as part of the CrossCity X5 service from Cardiff, for which it is route branded. The X5 ran in competition with Newport and Cardiff Bus, offering residents of Ringland and Newport East a through service to the capital.

YN54 AOF holds fleet number 46 despite being covered by a 'Movember' moustache on the front of the bus in this 10 November 2012 shot. It is numerically the last of the 54-registered Scania OmniCity buses.

A shot of Scania OmniCity YN57 FZP (47) wearing the then standard livery with 'unigo' branding, promoting Newport's student bus service. The company was entered into the UK Bus Awards for this in 2012 under the 'Innovation' category, which ironically was sponsored by Alexander Dennis. It is passing the water feature on the riverfront on the approach to Newport Bus Station on 11 May 2013. It is one of nine 57-plate examples in the fleet.

Scania OmniCity YN07 VCL (49) is seen on the end of its journey on service 42 from Moorland Park. It is passing preserved Leyland National 2 BUH 240V, which was new as National Welsh NS8012 in May 1980. With other preserved vehicles, the Leyland National was making its way to the depot of Cardiff Bus, who were marking the thirtieth anniversary of being a council-owned arm's-length company on 28 April 2018.

On the last day of December 2009, YN57 FZS (52) is seen wearing its traditional fleet livery with branding for the X30 express motorway service between Newport and Cardiff. It is in Cardiff Bus Station about to operate a return trip to its home city in December 2009. The X30 received refreshed route branding on delivery of the 2011 batch of Scania OmniCity buses worn by 110–112 inclusive.

Scania OmniCity CA52 JKK (57) is seen in May 2013 having worked Bettws Circular service 15. This area was used as an alighting-only point to save buses pulling up onto a stand in the bus station. Overtaking is newer Scania OmniCity YN57 FZR (50).

On 20 January 2007, CA52 JKN (58) is captured on service 17 to Foxgloves. It is one of six 52-plate examples, numbered 53–58 inclusively.

On 31 December 2009, Scania OmniCity YV03 PZR (61) is captured looking like a wrapped Christmas present as it exits the bus station on the 8A service to Ringland. 61 and 62 were the only 03-plate examples in the fleet delivered in August 2003; the other examples delivered that year received 53-plates.

On 3 November 2013, Scania OmniCity YV03 PZR (61) is seen in the High Street working a 28 service to Caerleon complete with a 'Movember' moustache.

YV03 PZR (61) is captured in use as a training vehicle in the bus station on 10 June 2022.

Scania OmniCity YV03 PZS (62) passes Newport railway station on Queensway, B4591, on 12 September 2014. It carries the name 'Lance Corporal Charles Jones', a former employee who served as a lance corporal in the 2nd Battalion of the Monmouthshire Regiment. Five OmniCitys in total received names in recognition of five Newport Corporation employees who were killed during the First World War.

A rear shot of YV03 PZS (62) showing the 'We will remember them' back applied to many similar vehicles in the fleet.

Optare Solo YJ57 YCH is in its Rail Linc livery for service 907 between Rogerstone and Newport railway stations. Although not showing a fleet number here, it carried fleet numbers 69 and 74 at separate times during its stay in the Newport Bus fleet. The change occurred after an incident whereby the bus, whilst operating the X16 (Risca to Cardiff), ended up down the railway bank adjacent to what is now Pye Corner station in Rogerstone.

A 5 November 2011 shot of Optare Solo YJ57 YCK (70). It is at the bottom of Stow Hill in the city centre having worked the Gaer Circular service 2A.

Optare Solo YJ08 PKO (73) leaves the bus station on service 9 to Langstone Business Park on 12 June 2010. Newport took six Optare Solos. Three had 57 plates (68–70) and were delivered in February 2008, with the remainder being 08 plates (71–73) and delivered in April 2008.

Scania N113CRL with Alexander Strider bodywork N78 PDW (78) is seen at the Market Square Bus Station on 27 February 2010, by this time wearing white with a dark green skirt without the 'N' roundel and dark rear. The advert on the third window from the rear was applied to many buses in the fleet in PSV driver recruitment attempts. A similar Alexander Strider is behind in the older fleet livery.

A fair number of Alexander Striders in the Newport fleet received three-quarter or all-over advertisements in the years that they operated for the company. One example is N83 PDW (83), seen in a three-quarter wrap for Newport City Homes. It awaits its next duty in Newport Bus Station on 22 March 2010.

On 4 June 2011, N83PDW (83) is captured wearing a hybrid livery – likely to be the case after the removal of its three-quarter wrap. The contrast between the white and cream with the green skirt is quite significant here.

Alexander ALX200-bodied Dennis Dart Y84 GBO (84) is seen operating service 17 to Folxgloves via Mount Pleasant on 2 July 2007.

Scania Strider P190 VDW (90) is captured in Cwmbran on 11 November 2010. It passes Alexander PS-bodied Volvo B10M M762 LAX (20362) in the Stagecoach South Wales fleet, both types considered to be great work horses of their era. Thirty of the type were delivered new to Newport between 1993 and 1997.

Alexander Strider-bodied Scania P91 VDW (91) enters the bus station in this shot from 29 December 2010.

W195 VWO (95) is numerically first of the five W-registered Alexander ALX200-bodied Dennis Dart SLFs, the others being W96 VWO (96), W97 VWO (97), W98 VWO (98) and W199 VWO (99). W195 VWO (95) is seen in High Street after completing service 17 from Malpas on 16 February 2014.

A shot taken on 19 January 2013 of ALX200-bodied Dennis Dart W97 VWO (97) covered in snow at the bus station with Enviro400 404 behind.

Alexander ALX200-bodied Dennis Dart SLF W199 VWO (99) is the last numerically of the type. It is seen turning into the old bus station on 18 May 2012.

Three of the MAN Wright Meridan buses are captured in storage in the MAN dealership on 21 January 2010 prior to them being received by Newport Bus. They entered service in the revised fleet colours, rendering this as a rather unique capture.

Numerically the first of the batch of six, with fleet number 101, MAN Wright Meridan CN60 FBO is seen alongside the daffodils nearing the end of its trip on service 42 from Spytty Park on St David's Day, 1 March, in 2013. The *Steel Wave* is seen behind.

Captured passing Scania OmniCity YN57 FZW (4) at the depot on 8 April 2021, Wright Meridan CN60 FBO (101) is in Newport County black and amber colours.

CN60 FBV (102) is captured turning right onto the Kingsway A4042 on 6 July 2013 having worked service 43 from Moorland Park. Behind the camera is the Riverfront performing arts theatre.

In all-over green livery, CN60 FBY (104) is seen on the A48 Southern Distributor Road working service 42 on 25 February 2022. The taking of this photograph was made easier by slow-moving traffic on the approach to one of the many roundabouts in the area.

CN60FBX (106) is seen on 11 May 2013 at the fountains outside Friars Walk on the end of its journey on service 17.

The first numerically of eight 11-plate Scania OmniCitys is 110, YT11 LUL. It is seen departing Spytty Retail Park for the city centre in March 2020 wearing an all-over wrap advertising the government scheme that allowed those aged between sixteen and twenty-one to save money on bus travel in Wales. When new, it was one of three to wear the updated X30 Newport to Cardiff express livery; the others were YT11 LUO (111) and YT11 LUP (112).

Scania OmniCity YT11 LUO (111) is captured on driver instruction duties exiting the bus station on 7 August 2024. It was repurposed for such duties following its active life as a public service vehicle. Like 110 and 112, it was new in X30 livery.

On 25 June 2011, YT11LUP (112) is seen entering the bus station having worked an X30 service from Cardiff for which it is branded. In September 2012 it would partake in the Driver of the Year event in Blackpool alongside other visiting vehicles from various UK fleets.

A shot of Scania Omicity YT11 LUD (113) on 13 June 2011 when nearly new. It is seen resting in the bus station. On 12 May 2012, the bus suffered a fire while operating on the X30 on the M4 between junctions 26 and 27 just before 5.30 p.m. After being refurbished it re-entered service, albeit in the revised lighter green and white Newport livery.

YT11 LUH (116) is captured in the Newport Depot in the company of YN54 AOD (44) amongst others on 19 December 2020.

Scania OmniCitys 110–117 were among the last OmniCity saloons completed for the UK market. On 27 March 2023, YT11 LUJ (117) is captured on the 26C to St Julians as it navigates the Old Green Roundabout before heading over Newport Bridge.

Seventeen-seat Mercedes-Benz Sprinter BL16 FZK (218) is seen in Newport having arrived into the city's Market Square Bus Station on a 31 DRT service on 7 August 2020. DRT is a Demand Responsive Transport service whereby users can pre-book travel with the benefit of commercial bus ticketing in operation. It was one of three identical vehicles used for this purpose at the time, the others being BL16 FZM (216) and BL16 FZJ (217).

Numerous Ford Transit Minibuses have been operated by Newport Bus with a mix of 66, 17, 67, 18, 21 and 24 plate registrations and fleet numbers ranging between 220 and 243. The majority of these were white, with exception of examples such as HK67 EFD (220), HV18 GVP (226) and HV18 GVO (227) in silver. The latter is seen here resting in the bus station on 7 August 2020. A few of these vehicles were used on an NHS staff contract along with other private work. Its fleet number is displayed beneath the wing mirror.

White Ford Transit Minibus YS21 JUX (234) is captured on 6 May 2022 on the raised curb often used as a parking area for ancillary and small vehicles in the bus station, to the right of the exit.

Mercedes-Benz Sprinters RJ21 UZA (244) and RJ21 UYZ (246) are captured in the entrance to Market Square Bus Station on 10 June 2022 on DRT services. RJ21 UZG has fleet number 245. The trio were plain white, whereas similar examples that followed were in Fflecsi red and silver for that initiative. RO21 ODT (252) and RO21 WDN (253) stayed in the fleet beyond Fflecsi.

Fflecsi-branded EVM-bodied Mercedes-Benz Sprinter RO21 TZG (250) is captured resting in the entrance of Market Square Bus Station on 6 May 2022.

Alexander Royale-bodied Volvo Olympian P272 PSX (272) was new to Lothian Buses in July 1997. It is seen on 31 December 2009 about to operate a service 30 from the capital to Newport. Upon leaving the Newport fleet it passed to M Travel of Castleford, where it operated in Newport colours until repainted into their livery during 2015. These vehicles were a surprising addition to the Newport fleet, being high-floor and to dual-door configuration with traditional-style destination blinds.

Three Alexander Royale-bodied Volvo Olympians stand in the yard of the Corporation Road Depot. From left to right are P283 PSX (283), P276 PSX (276) and P268 PSX (268). Also alongside is native Newport ALX400-bodied Dennis Trident V35 HTG (35).

P279 PSX (279) is captured leaving the bus station on 2 June 2012 on service 44. Six arrived at Newport in 2009 and lasted in the fleet until 2013.

Newport took seventeen Alexander Dennis Enviro200s in 2011 and 2012. Exemplifying the shorter 8.9-m version, YX11 CRK (301) is captured in Greyfriars Road, Cardiff, having worked the X16 service from Risca on 29 November 2012.

In recognition of key workers during the pandemic, Alexander Dennis Enviro200 YX11 AGY (304) is seen wearing a rear wrap with the 'Stay Safe' message. It is resting in Friars Walk Bus Station on 19 December 2020.

YX11 AGZ (305) is pulling out of the archway at the exit of Monmouth Bus Station on local service W5 on 17 October 2013 in the livery that was applied to most examples from new.

Wearing it's black and amber Newport County colours, Alexander Dennis Enviro200 YX11 AHV (306) is captured on 17 August 2022 on service 20C to Spytty Retail Park. The *Steel Wave* is evident in the background as the bus waits at the lights on the Old Green Roundabout.

Alexander Dennis Enviro200 YX61 DVT (307) is captured on 17 October 2020 laying over in Newport Bus Station with its rear advertisement encouraging motorists to 'make the switch' to public transport. It was this bus that was formerly adorned with an all-over wrap showing poppies and soldier silhouettes and 'We Will Remember Them' messaging on the rear. This bus later passed to Notts & Derby, obtaining fleet number 54.

YX61 DVU (308) is seen in Usk Square collecting customers bound for Newport whilst on service 60 on 2 August 2016.

Supplementing 301–309, YX12 DME (310) is one of two 12-plate 8.9-m Alexander Dennis Enviro200 examples (the other being YX12 DMF, 311) new to Newport in 2012 with revised headlight styling. The offside emergency exit is on the lower part of the saloon, unlike 301–309. This shot is from 8 February 2013 in Chepstow Bus Station.

In all-over green, YX12 DHM (312) awaits its next turn of duty in the depot on 8 April 2021. Numerically, it forms the first of five similar vehicles in the fleet with the longer 10.8-m Alexander Dennis Enviro200 bodywork.

Seen on 17 October 2020 is YX12 DHO (314) in all-over green livery with the Pride stripe and Newport Bus logo on display as it comes to the end of service 19E. Other vehicles similarly wore this Pride branding around the same time.

YX12 DHP (315) is seen when brand new on 28 April 2012 about to operate service 1 to Wern Industrial Estate in Rogerstone. Again, all later received full fleet livery but initially operated in plain white with decals applied, as seen here.

YX12 DHV (317) was one of the buses lost in an arson attack at the depot on 3 December 2012. It is seen in Newport Bus Station on 4 August 2012 branded for the Heath Park and Ride, the route where it spent the majority of its short working life.

YX13 EGC (318) is one of two 13-plate 8.9-m Alexander Dennis Enviro200 examples new to Newport with tinted windows and to full Newport Bus internal specification – the other earlier Enviro200s were built to dealer stock specification. It is seen outside the Admiral Building on 5 November 2013 on service 74 to Chepstow. Both 318 and 319 (registered YX13 EGD) were intended for dedicated use on the Chepstow town services, as per the branding on view here.

On service 1 to Wern Industrial Estate in Rogerstone is YX61 DOU displaying fleet number 320 on 24 June 2013. It is seen climbing Stow Hill on its way out of the city. It retained its 'Next generation Enviro200' demonstration livery for the entire time it was in Newport. It later passed to Faresaver of Chippenham. It had unusual mustard and maroon high-backed seats.

Two non-native 8.9-m Alexander Dennis Enviro200s stayed permanently within the Newport Bus fleet after a period of time on loan. MX09 MHY became 321 and MX09 MHZ became 322 yet were initially numbered 222 and 333 respectively whilst on loan. Both previously operated on Metro Shuttle (Manchester) free bus services. 321 is captured in all-over white with fleet number (222) on 9 March 2013 in the bus station.

MX09 MHZ (322) is captured in the bus station on 3 June 2020.

Newport were late adopters of the Transbus Dart SLF, with fourteen second-hand examples appearing during 2014 to assist in the company meeting DDA regulations and replacing older stock. Many other Welsh operators had Dennis Dart SLF Pointer 2s/Alexander Dennis Darts in the fleet for some years prior and they became a common sight in Welsh towns, cities and countryside. KP02 PWU, with fleet number 326, is seen in Market Square Bus Station on 26 October 2015.

Transbus Dart SLF KU52 YKP (329) is captured on 28 April 2018 on service 6A, whilst similar KU02 YUD (331) is in pursuit working a Gaer service. Newport took fourteen examples (323–336), converting most to single-door layout.

KU52 YKV (332) is captured returning to the bus station after having worked service 6A on 29 April 2017.

KU52 YKN (335) is seen resting in the bus station on 29 March 2021. As well as the 'Thank you NHS' message on one of its nearside windows, it also displays the National Day of Reflection flower for Tuesday 23 March to reflect on our collective loss, to support those who've been bereaved, and hope for a brighter future after the coronavirus pandemic.

Alexander Dennis Enviro200 MMC SK24 CWA (337) is captured navigating the roundabout after serving the Morrisons store in Rogerstone on 17 August 2024. It is one of six with Newport Bus, numbered 337 to 342.

Alexander Dennis Enviro200 MMC SK24 CWC (338) is captured on the R1 service at the Tesco store in Pontymister on 6 July 2024.

Alexander Dennis Enviro200 MMC YX74 OOH (342) is captured working the 69 service to Monmouth on 15 November 2025 in Chepstow Bus Station. It is numerically the last of six similar vehicles that entered the fleet in 2024, numbered 337 to 342 inclusively.

Two Volvo B8RLE MCV Evoras, BV19LPA (351) and BV19 LPC (352), were surprising additions to the fleet and both took their numbers from the Stagecoach fleet numbering system (21351 and 21352) where they were operated both prior and subsequent to Newport Bus. They were for use on the Traws Cymru T7 service, linking Magor with Chepstow, Cribbs Causeway and Bristol. The former is pictured resting in the depot on 8 April 2021 alongside Scania OmniCity YT11 LUL (110).

In Traws Cymru livery for the T7 service, Yutong E12 CE72 YRL (355) is captured in Cheptsow Bus Station on 15 November 2025. It is one of two operated by Newport in this livery, the other being CE72 YRM (354), that have full panelling around the batteries unlike Newport's green examples.

Five Alexander Dennis Enviro400s entered the Newport Bus fleet in November 2012 numbered 400–404 – the latter had tables on the top deck and featured in the 2012 Euro Bus Expo at the NEC, Birmingham. Three out of the five are captured in Newport Bus Station on 16 March 2013. SN62 AOO (401) leads SN62 AOP (402) and SN62 AOW (403) in the line-up here.

Alexander Dennis Enviro400 SN62 AOO (401) is captured exiting Jubilee Park in Rogerstone on service 1 on 9 January 2023. Welsh street artist Tee2Sugars was commissioned to paint the vehicle to honour local art, key figures and the history of the city. Its offside features the Chartist movement with 'Strive for better' wording, as captured here.

The nearside of 401 displays Margaret Haig Thomas, or Lady Rhondda, and depictions of Newport trams, as captured here on 7 August 2024 in Newport Bus Station. 'Ymdrechu am well' translates to 'Strive for better' as per the offside.

On 12 June 2022, SN62 AOP (422) is captured at the Barry Festival of Transport wearing its Ukraine-flag-inspired wrap with the wording 'Supporting the People of Ukraine'.

Alexander Dennis Enviro400 SN62AOW (403) entering Newport Bus Station to commence service JF1 to John Frost School on 9 September 2019. It wears Coleg Gwent 'Made for Greatness' three-quarter wrap, with the offside in Welsh.

On 15 December 2021, SN62 AOW (403) is seen exiting the bus station wearing a striking Christmas wrap working the 8C to Ringland. This was the first Christmas livery since the application to YX11 AGY (304) in 2012, but it continued a long tradition of festive designs on Newport buses.

SN62 AOW (403) is seen leaving Friars Walk Bus Station on 10 June 2022 wearing its Platinum Jubilee livery. Its nearside reads 'Congratulations to Her Majesty The Queen on Her Platinum Jubilee from Her Golden Jubilee City, 1952–2002'. The offside included this in Welsh. Newport had gained city status twenty years prior in 2002 during the year of Elizabeth II's Golden Jubilee.

On 18 November 2021, SN62 AOX (404) is captured outside Crosskeys College helping to promote jobs with the NHS and Aneurin Bevan University Health Board.

Alexander Dennis Enviro400 SN62 AOX (404) is captured entering the bus station having worked the 74A service from Underwood on 7 October 2022. It is wearing an all-over wrap for Cancer Research Wales.

Alexander Dennis Enviro400 MMC SK70 BUO (405) is captured on service 26C to St Julians on 5 November 2021. It is one of three similar vehicles taken into stock in February 2021, having been delivered at the end of 2020, the other two being SK70 BUP (406) and SK70 OLA (407). Further similar examples were new to Newport – SK71 CKL (410), YX72 ONR (411) and YX72 ONU (417).

A rear shot taken on 17 August 2022 of Alexander Dennis Enviro400 MMC SK70 BUO (405) and Alexander Dennis Enviro400 SN62 AOH (400) to allow for a comparison of the development of the type. 400 is wearing a rear advert for KLA ('Keep Looking Ahead') careers.

YX70 OLA (407) is seen approaching Newport Bus Station on 29 March 2021 having completed a trip on service 42 from Newport Retail Park.

Retaining dual-door configuration after a repaint, non-native Alexander Dennis Enviro400 LK55 KKO (408) sits alongside another non-native double-decker, Alexander ALX400 Dennis Trident KV02 URL (428), in the Newport Bus Depot on 8 April 2021. 408 was new to Metroline with fleet number TE680, whereas 428 was new to Connex Bus with fleet number TA103.

Scania OmniCity YT09 ZTL (412) is captured in the bus station not in service on 21 June 2023. It was one of five examples that entered the fleet numbered 412–416, this example being the only 09 plate and the others being 59-plate examples. All were new to London United and operated in white with Newport fleet names.

Alexander Dennis Enviro400 MMC YX72 ONU (417) is captured at the terminus of service 1 at Morrisons in Rogerstone on 17 March 2023. Unlike 405, 406, 407 and 410, 411 and 417 did not have the 'Greener, Smarter, Safer' vinyls applied. Incidentally, 417 was the 'Christmas Bus' for 2024, having 'Experience Newport this Christmas' vinyls applied between the decks and snowflakes applied elsewhere across its bodywork.

On 8 June 2025, CK24 AUH (418) is captured at Barry Island at the Festival of Transport. It is one of two Yutong U11DDs in the fleet. Newport was the first operator in the UK to receive this vehicle type. It is pictured alongside LN51 XKR (420) and YT11 LUO (111).

CK24AUO (419) is captured exiting the bus station on the 30 to Cardiff on 7 August 2024.

On 11 August 2013, Plaxton President-bodied Transbus Trident LN51 KXR (420) is pictured leaving the bus station on service 8C to Ringland. It is one of six of the type entering the Newport fleet in 2013 via Ensign Bus. All had been new to Metroline and received single-door conversions. 420 held fleet number TPL238 with Metroline.

Leaving the bus station on 17 September 2013 is Plaxton President LR02 BAO (423). It's yet to receive its vinyls at this stage. The double-deck livery it would receive was introduced in 2011. 423 was formerly Metroline's SEL744.

LR02 BAU (424) is captured exiting the bus station on Bettws Circular service 16 on 17 August 2022 wearing the later all-over green livery. 424 was new to Metroline as their SEL745.

Alexander Dennis ALX400 KN52 NDY (434) is captured in the bus station on 19 July 2021. Yutong E12 YD70 CFG (Z04) is passing on the 8C service to Ringland. Thirteen examples of the type were acquired by Newport in 2017 numbered 426–437, with 440 being acquired in 2018. 433–437 were initially numbered 1007, 1009, 1002, 1008 and 1001 respectively.

LR52 LYC, with fleet number 438, is one of two East Lancs Myllennium Lolyne-bodied Dennis Tridents to be operated by Newport Bus – the other being LR52 LWF, numbered 439. They arrived second-hand from CT Plus as their HTL12/7 to Newport during mid-2017 and were initially numbered 1006 and 1004 respectively. A model of this vehicle in its red CT Plus livery was produced by Corgi Original Omnibus, numbered OM42513 and released in October 2005. 438 is seen in the company of various other vehicles in the fleet at the depot on 8 April 2021.

LR52 LWF (439) is captured in the bus station on 15 June 2022 working the 26A to St Julians. This example ran in service with Newport Bus in its former red livery and in dual-door configuration when initially transferred to Newport in 2017.

Seen exiting the bus station on 3 June 2020 is Alexander ALX400-bodied Dennis Trident KV02URM (440) on service 6E to Ringland. It first operated for Connex with fleet number TA104 before passing to Travel London, becoming their 9804. It operated for Thurmaston Bus and later Yorkshire Tiger in Dawson Bus and Coach Rental dealer white before coming to Newport.

Yutong E12 YK66 CBC became Z01 in the Newport fleet in 2018, having previously being used as a demonstrator. It is captured on 3 June 2020 approaching the bus station wearing 'ride the first fully electric bus in Wales' vinyls. When new, it wore Arriva livery and operated with their North West division with fleet number 7911 before being on demonstration with various other operators in plain white.

Yutong E12 YD70 CFJ (Z05) is seen operating the 36 to Duffryn on 5 November 2021, with identical YJ70 CFE (Z02) having worked service 27 from Caerleon. Fourteen native 70-plate Yutong E12s were new to Newport in 2020.

Yutong E12 YD70 CFK (Z06) is captured on 17 October 2020 working its way back to the bus station after having worked the 27 service from Caerleon.

On 4 March 2022, YD70 CFL (Z07) is pictured passing the *Steel Wave* after having worked the X30 service from Cardiff.

Yutong E12 YD70 CHJ is seen waiting to exit the bus station on 17 October 2020 whilst working the 74A service to Underwood. This bus later received the name 'Edwin Marsh' in recognition of the former MD of Newport Transport who led the municipal between 1988 and 2001. Marsh passed away on 21 April 2023, aged eighty-three.

Yutong E12 YD70 CHL is captured outside the Tesco Extra store in Spytty on 17 April 2021.

YD70 CHL (Z13) is captured passing Newport cenotaph on 1 November 2025. The cenotaph was unveiled by Lord Tredegar in June 1923 to commemorate the local people who died in active service in the First World War. It now also commemorates people who died in subsequent wars.

Two identical Yutong E12s seen in Newport Bus Station on 17 October 2020: YD70 CHN (Z14) about to operate service 42 and YD70CHJ (Z11) about to operate the 74A. The round vinyl near the rear right light clusters indicate how many electric vehicles are in the fleet. For example, Z14 reads 'I am electric bus 14/15' – correct at the time of capture.

Yutong E10 YG18 CVS was loaned as a demonstrator from around April 2020 until it became a permanent member of the fleet from late 2020. It is captured passing Clarence House in full Newport livery on 17 March 2023 having worked the 8A from Ringland. One of the distinguishable features of this bus making it different from the other native examples is the split destination display.

On display on the Pelican Yutong stand at the Euro Bus Expo at the NEC in 2022 is Yutong E10 CE22 WWT (Z23). Also visible alongside is a Traws Cymru-liveried Yutong E12. Newport's Isuzu AOS Grand Touro KX72 CWO (D20) was also on display at this event.

Yutong E10 CE22 WWN (Z24), carrying the name 'C.R. Yalland R.N', is captured in Lydney working service 73 to Chepstow. Lydney is one of the most easterly services operated by Newport Bus, covering Chepstow, Tutshill, Woolaston, Alvington, Aylburton, Lydney station, Blakeney, Dean Heritage Centre, Soudley, Ruspidge, Cinderford, Forest of Dean Community Hospital, Mitcheldean and Gloucestershire College.

Yutong E10 CE22 WWO (Z26) is pictured crossing Newport Bridge with elaborate lamp posts towards Clarence Place on 1 November 2025 whilst working the 73 service to Chepstow. There are seventeen native Yutong E10s: Z21, Z23–31, Z33–39, the latter being 23-plates though they formally carried 22-plates when new.

Yutong E10 CE22 WWR (Z27) is captured working service 60 from Monmouth on 7 October 2022. It is navigating the roundabout at Queensway to serve Newport station, with the exit for Bridge Street to left of the rear of the bus. As above, various similar vehicles received names in recognition of those who served and lost their lives in the two world wars, Z27 receiving the name 'R. J. Wilkins RE'.

Yutong E12 CE22 WXF (Z32) is captured on Greyfriars Road, Cardiff, having worked the X30 service from Newport on 18 July 2025.

CK24 AVL (Z34) is one of eleven Yutong E9Ls at Newport numbered between Z34 and Z55. It is captured outside the home of the Cardiff Transport Preservation Group at 'the Bus Depot', Barry, on 8 September 2024, an event that focused on Newport Bus and its heritage.

Yutong E9L CK24 AVP (Z46) is captured at Tesco in Pontymister on the R2 service.

CK24 AWH is seen on 7 June 2024 in the entrance to Market Square Bus Station with its destination set for the 31A to Marshfield.

Yutong E9L CE224 AUU (Z52) is captured leaving the bus station on 7 August 2024 working service 20 to Newport Retail Park.

CK24 AVF (Z54) is captured in Risca on 5 April 2024. This and other examples were pressed into service without vinyls, as evident here. It's captured in Risca having worked the R1 from Newport after having taken over the service from Stagecoach in South Wales.

Newport Coach

A line-up of Scania K91B1s with Irizar bodywork are captured resting between school duties at the Newport Depot on 14 May 2010. These were used on school services being endorsed by 'Belt Up School Kids' (BUSK). All were disposed of by Newport, so it was a surprise when YN54 OCE (23) re-entered the fleet from Ashwood Travel, High Wycombe, as D52 during 2023 together with similar YN56 FEX (D46) and YN56 FEV (D49), both from Turners, Bristol.

Isuzu AOS Grand Touro KX72 CWO (D20) was displayed at the 2022 Euro Bus Expo in the NEC. It wasn't the only Newport vehicle in the show that year; Yutong E10 CE22 WWT (Z23) was on display on the Pelican Yutong stand.

Plaxton Panther-bodied Volvo B12B YN06 MXV was new to Wooton's in April 2006. It was acquired by Newport Transport in May 2012 and named 'Olivia' as an identifier alongside fleet number 27. It is seen resting in the Newport Depot on 19 September 2020 with YN06 MXU, named 'Sophie', visible behind. They later wore the all-over green livery.

KX59DLU (29) and SV59CHL (28) sit alongside each other in the depot on 19 September 2020. These Volvo B12Bs with Plaxton Panther bodywork were new to Stagecoach, though were acquired by Newport to support the growing private-hire function, forming the first tri-axles in the fleet.

Plaxon Elite-bodied Volvo B9R YN10 FZT (D30) entered the Newport fleet in November 2022 from Cymru Coaches, though was new to Logan of Dunloy (Northern Ireland) in May 2010. It is captured in the grounds of Rogerstone Primary School on 11 July 2025.

Van-Hool Alizee-bodied DAFSB4000 WT54 JAC (D31) is captured in the depot on 4 September 2025. It passed to Newport from Eagle Coaches during January 2023, though was new to Wicksons of Walsall Wood in September 2004.

Yutong TCe12 CE23 ZDK (D32) is captured in the depot on 13 November 2025. It is one of four new to Newport in June 2023 (D32–35) and reported in the news as Wales's first battery-electric coaches. They are PSVAR compliant with dual doors, forty-six seats and a toilet onboard.

Yutong TCe12 CE23 ZDJ (D43) is captured in its Flixbus livery at Morrisons in Rogerstone working a works service for a nearby food manufacturer. The livery was applied in February 2024, with the vehicle being deployed on the Flixbus network between Newport, Bristol and London for a trial period between 21 March and June that year. At the London end, the coach was scheduled to be charged at Transport UK London Bus Depot (formally known as Abellio) in Battersea prior to its return trip back to Wales. It was marked as the first electric long-distance coach service in England and Wales.

Newport received eight Volvo 9700 B13Rs for use on Flixbus services. BV23NNJ (D42) is captured outside Newport station at the Flixbus stop on 30 December 2023.

Plaxton Panther-bodied Volvo B12B FJ55 DZL (D51) is captured resting at the depot on 4 September 2025. It was new to Silverdale of Nottingham as a National Express vehicle. It served with various other operators before entering the Newport fleet from Ashwood Travel, High Wycombe, during May 2023.

CK24 AWJ (D56), captured in the depot on 13 November 2025, is one of seven Yutong GT12s branded for Flixbus services. They were new in June 2024. Similar CK73 ATY (D50) wears the Flixbus base colour with the Newport Coach fleet name.

Demonstrators and Loan Vehicles

Many demonstrators have been trialled at Newport Bus. Here is just a sample. On 16 August 2010, Alexander Dennis Enviro400 demonstrator SN59 AWX is captured in Newport Bus Station on service 30 to Cardiff. It would later end up in the fleet of McGill's, Greenock.

Scania OmniLink demonstrator YS10 XBO is being pursued out of the old bus station by native Alexander Strider N180 PDW (80) whilst operating on the 8 to Ringland in September 2010. It is in plain white livery with 'Scania Euro 5 EEV Engine' lettering. It later passed to Wessex Connect, Bristol.

Scania Omnilink demonstrator LT11 LPN is captured in the bus station on 17 June 2011 working service 36 to Celtic Springs. It later became a permanent member of the Xelabus fleet, Eastleigh.

A loan vehicle from Scania Bus and Coach rather than a demonstrator, Scania OmniCity YN54 AHP spent a period of time with Newport Bus whilst 113 was being repaired. It was Nottingham City Transport's 216. It is captured leaving the bus station on 14 July 2012 whilst working the 8A to Ringland.

Mercedes-Benz Citaro BF60 OEZ is seen on loan with Newport Bus on 4 August 2012. It was also used in service with Stagecoach in South Wales on their X24 service from Cwmbran Depot as well as other Welsh operators. It later passed to the Your Bus fleet in Nottingham.

Seen on 9 November 2012, having worked the X30 service from Newport, is Scania OmniCity demonstrator YT11 LSE. It would later find a home in West Coast Motors. Around this time it was rumoured that a batch were ordered by Newport, but these did not materialise.

Scania K230UB Alexander Dennis Enviro300 YN62 AAK was on loan to Newport Bus as a demonstrator during December 2012. It is seen in Newport Bus Station in its silver demonstrator livery. It later passed to Midland Classic of Burton-upon-Trent.

The first gas-powered demonstrator bus to be built by ADL and Scania, Scania K270UB Alexander Dennis Enviro300SG demonstrator YT13 YUK is seen in September 2013 exiting Newport Bus Station on the 8C to Ringland. The vehicle would later receive a Bio Bus all-over wrap and operated for First Bristol with fleet number 68501 and later Reading Buses with registration BU52 GAS (435).

Another demonstrator powered by natural gas trialled by Newport Bus is Caetano MAN EcoCity WX13 GHN, seen operating the X30 to Cardiff on 8 April 2013. It later entered the fleet of Arriva North East as their 4814.

Seen on 11 March 2017 in Market Square Bus Station is DF66 AEC, a Mercedes-Benz Mellor demonstrator being used on DRT services. It later entered the fleet of PC Coaches of Lincoln. When new it was displayed at the 2016 Euro Bus Expo at the NEC as a new entrant to the market.

Yutong E10 YG18 CVS is captured on 3 June 2020 working the 28 service to Caerleon. It wears its red London livery worn from new. It was displayed at 'Coach and Bus UK' at the NEC in 2018. Before its arrival at Newport, it operated for various other companies including Metroline London, Abellio London, Tower Transit, CT Plus, Arriva London, Arriva Midlands, First West Yorkshire and Diamond Bus North West.

Prior to the entry of Newport's native Yutong U11DDs, Pelican demonstrator UU11 DDD was loaned to Newport. It is captured at the depot on 3 February 2024.

Some Ex-Newport Transport Preserved Buses

Preserved Alexander-bodied Leyland Atlantean PDR1/1 EDW 68D was new in March 1966 as Newport's 68 – one of the first rear-engined buses to enter service. It forms part of the Cardiff Transport Preservation Group's collection of vehicles. Similar PDW 98H is thought to still be in existence after non-PSV use as a burger bar.

Alexander RH-bodied Scania 113DRB F41 YHB is captured in Barry Island wearing its full Newport City Sightseeing livery at the Festival of Transport on 10 June 2018. It was new to Newport Transport in November 1988.

F41 YHB is captured exiting 'the Bus Depot', Barry, on 7 September 2025. It has been restored into its green and cream livery by the group and has appropriate Newport Transport vinyls. It retains its open-top configuration, with its Newport City Sightseeing red seating replaced with green covering. Note that although authentic looking, the destination display '30 Newport' is a vinyl replica and not a true roller bind.

Longwell Green-bodied Leyland Titan PD2 PDW 484 (178) is captured approaching 'the Bus Depot', Barry, on 7 September 2025 having been on a free ride around the town, made famous by the much-loved and award-winning *Gavin and Stacey* series.

Metro-Scania YDW 756K (56) was one of sixteen new to Newport in July 1972. Other examples entered the fleet from London, which were PGC 201/3-6L (101/3–6), though 101 did not enter service. 756 is captured in the depot on 13 November 2025. Sister vehicle YDW 758K resides with the Cardiff Transport Preservation Group.

A surprise survivor rather than one that had reached preservation at the time the photo was taken on 15 November 2025. Alexander-bodied Scania N112 B223 YUH (23) stands in a sorry state in a vehicle compound in one of the industrial areas of the city in the livery of TRC Coaches of Treorchy, where it most recently operated.

Bus Interiors

Interior of one of the ex-Lothian Alexander Royale-bodied Volvo Olympians. Whilst some received the seats from Newport's native ALX400s when they received refurbishments themselves, some retained Lothian's interiors, with the tartan-inspired moquette being indicative of their place of origin.

Interior shot of the upstairs of a native Newport Bus Alexander Dennis Enviro400 with high-back seating and seatbelts. Note the Newport Bus logo pressed into the headrests.

Interior shot of a Newport Bus Yutong E12. This specification was consistent in all Yutong bus deliveries, making all vehicles unmistakably 'Newport Bus'.

Interior shot of Newport Bus Yutong E10 YG18 CVS (Z16) with dual-door arrangement and blue seating prior to conversion to single-door layout and interior refurbishment into Newport Bus specification.

Interior shot of YG18 CVS (Z16) after refurbishment and the removal of its centre door.

Upstairs shot of a Plaxton President-bodied Dennis Trident, which were refurbished prior to entry into service with Newport into this specification.

Interior downstairs shot of Yutong U11DD CK24 AUH (418).

Upstairs interior shot of LJ56 VTO (409), which retains its red moquette from Abellio London.

Upstairs interior shot of LR52 LYC (438).

Interior shot of a Wright Meridian captured with the moquette that was once fleet standard.

Interior shot of Scania OmniCity YN54 AOA (41). Various vehicles received this updated interior moquette, which became standard on new vehicles for a period of time.

Interior shot of Scania OmniCity YT11LUL (110), allowing for a comparison of revised styling between different-aged Scania OmniCity buses in the fleet.

Interior shot of Scania OmniCity YN54AOC (43), which, like others, received two-tone grey seat coverings upon refurbishment in April 2021.

Interior shot of Alexander Dennis Enviro200 YX12 DHM (312) with its standard ADL dealer stock specification seating.

Interior shot (front to back) of short-wheelbase Alexander Dennis Enviro200 YX11 AGY (304), again with dealer stock specification, allowing a comparison to be drawn. Note the 'Thank you NHS' and 'Stay safe' messaging on the side and rear windows as well as Covid-19 seating restrictions on some seats.

Interior of preserved Metro-Scania YDW 756K (56) with seats and coving panels in good condition.

Bus Station and Depot

Above: A picture of the depot on Corporation Road taken on 13 November 2025. In the body shop and stores on-site, evidence of the tram tracks remain. The last tram service ran on 5 September 1937.

Right: A plaque on the wall in the reception of the depot on Corporation Road commemorating those who fell in action in the First and Second World Wars.

A June 2012 picture of seven unidentified Newport Bus rears. It was this top end of the bus station that Newport Bus occupied, with the lower end of the station being occupied by Stagecoach and other operators. The station was cosmetically refurbished prior to the Ryder Cup in 2010, though it closed for good in autumn 2013.

Inside the passenger area of the old Newport Bus Station looking towards bay 30. Heading straight on would lead you to the Newport Bus travel shop, newsagent, public convenience and drivers' room.

The demolition of the bus station is well underway in this image from November 2013.

Friars Walk Bus Station seen fully operational in September 2016. The bays are narrower than the previous station, meaning that buses are more compact whilst on stand. Nearest the camera is Scania OmniCity YT11 LUJ (117) with a rear 'we will remember them' vinyl.

Three Scania OmniCity buses from the 2011 delivery occupying bays 18 to 20 during January 2014.

The newly constructed Market Square Bus Station in December 2013. Criticism was received from customers that approaching vehicles could not be seen clearly through the panelling.